Echoes of Aztlán

*A Poetic Journey Through Race,
Culture, and Ancestry*

A companion book to
A Fly In Milk
(Una Mosca en la Leche)

Victor Vasquez

Copyright © 2025 Victor Vasquez

All Rights Reserved.

No content of this book may be copied, excerpted, replicated, or shared without the permission of the author.

Published by SuburbanBuzz.com LLC

ISBN: 978-1-959446-87-3

DEDICATION

To all the remarkable people who have shaped my journey, this book is dedicated to you.

From friends and family whose relationships enriched every stage of my life to those who nurtured my creative spirit, your influence has been profound. This collection of poems reflects my experiences growing up in the United States as a Mexican American with Indigenous roots—a tapestry woven with threads of identity, resilience, and cultural pride.

I was fortunate to grow up in a small town of just five thousand people, where everyone knew your name, your family, and even your evening plans. It was a community where accountability was shared, guidance was freely given, and every interaction played a role in shaping who I am today.

To that community and to all who inspired, supported, and believed in me—thank you. This book is a testament to your impact, and I am forever grateful for your time, kindness, and unwavering encouragement.

CONTENTS

ACKNOWLEDGMENTS i
INTRODUCTION 3
CHAPTER 1 We Are Home on Our Land 7
   The Impacts of Conquest 8
   The Truth 10
   Under an Aztec Sun 11
   The Mexican Eagle 12
   Sun of Life 14
   Raza is Born 15
CHAPTER 2 Identity 17
   In the Beets 19
   Mint Field 20
   Born in the Beets 22
   Eagles Pass 23
   Mestizo 24
   Hermiston 25
   Chicano Education 26
   Children 27
   The Crying Lady (La Llorona) 28
CHAPTER 3 The Uncle Factor 31
   American Aztec Warriors 35
   Orders 36
   Mexican-American Veteran 38
   Boy Soldiers 40
   Sunset 42
   Greyhound 44
   A Young Man Off to War 46
   Conflicted 48
   Resistance 49
CHAPTER 4 Formula for Rebellion 51
   Assimilation 53
   Remember the Revolution 54
   Pipeline 56
   Coldfoot Winter 58

CHAPTER 5 Thoughts of Love 61
　Almost Caught 66
　Free and Alone... 67
　A New Day.. 68
　Star My Friend... 69
　Plea for Love 70
　Alma... 71
　What Love is Built On... 72
　I Cielo 73
　In Silence.. 74
　Promise 75
　Are You Sure?.. 76
　The Light.. 78
　Aztec Princess 80
　Together Bound.. 81
　Valentine's Day 82
　Mi Vida... 83
　What's In a Southern Name?... 84
　When We Knew Each Other.. 86
　Seasons Change.. 87
　Mankind's Universe... 88
CHAPTER 6 What is Next? 91
　To Survive.. 94
　The Mother... 95
　Life 96
　Shadow of Wisdom 97
　Origins of Chicomoztoc 98
　Antiquity... 100
　Chicano of the Past 101
　Breaking News 102
　Time to Change.. 104
　Toward the Sun of Huitzilopochtli 106
　Daybreak 107
　Infinite 108
　Freedom Found 109
CONCLUSION.. 111
ABOUT THE AUTHOR 113

ACKNOWLEDGMENTS

This book would not have been possible without the unwavering support of my family, especially my wife. At every stage of this journey, I was fortunate to have the encouragement and thoughtful critiques of friends and family members who helped shape my work as it evolved. Their insights and feedback gave me the hope and determination to create a book that I aspire to be both informative and entertaining.

I am also profoundly grateful to my editor, Melanie Saxton, Holly Chervnsik of SuburbanBuzz Publishing, and Holly Lyn Walrath for their exceptional expertise, particularly in the art of writing poetry. Their invaluable guidance, editorial acumen, and steadfast dedication were crucial in bringing this project to life. Their professionalism and belief in this endeavor helped transform my creative vision into a reality.

To everyone who believed in this project and contributed to its success—thank you for helping me make this dream come true.

INTRODUCTION

In my autofiction, *A Fly in Milk*, I speak of the heart of the borderlands between the United States and Mexico, where the desert sun blazes fiercely. This is where my family's story took root. It is a tale embedded with an ancient heritage that blended into a common way of life, one challenged with contemporary struggles. Ours is the journey of a Mexican immigrant family bound by deep Aztec ancestry and driven by an unrelenting pursuit of economic justice, identity, and belonging. Along the way, our voices grew stronger, refusing to be silenced.

Our roots run deep in the fertile soil of the Valley of Mexico, where the remnants of Tenochtitlán, the ancient capital of the Aztec empire, still whisper to those who listen. My life is a testament to those origins, and the blood of warriors and poets runs through my veins.

I grew up immersed in the vibrancy of Mexico's Indigenous culture—the rhythmic chants of traditional songs, the murals depicting gods and heroes, and the stories that connected my people to our ancestral past. Yet, these cultural riches stood in stark contrast to the grinding poverty that defined our daily lives. My family were migrant farm workers, moving back and forth between Mexico and the western states of California, Oregon, and Washington.

Our journey north was not by choice. Like so many before us, my family fled the shadows of the Spanish conquest, searching for the elusive promise of El Norte. We crossed the border with hearts full of hope and only a few cherished possessions—a worn notebook of poems and sketches among them. But the land of opportunity proved far less welcoming than we imagined.

We faced the harsh realities of racial discrimination, language barriers, and the tension of a new culture that was both fascinating and alienating. The lush, expansive rural landscapes of places we traveled to were wide-open spaces with unfamiliar faces, far from the world of my tight-knit community on the border. Back home, everyone knew who you were; here, we were strangers—our faces, accents, and traditions betraying our Indigenous origins.

The weight of being seen as outsiders was heavy. We came from a history that blended Aztec roots with the blood of Spanish conquistadors, carrying the legacy of our ancestors in our language, culture, and skin. But in this new world, those legacies marked us as different, often unwelcome.

At school, I grappled with the sting of exclusion. My classmates mocked our food, our language, and our songs. Teachers overlooked the richness of our heritage, seeing only children who struggled with English. Yet, even as others sought to diminish it, our Aztec ancestry became a source of immense pride for me—a pillar of stability in an unsteady world.

In the quiet corners of labor camp cabins, amid the chaos of a family of six crammed into a single room, I found solace in poetry. I wrote about my dreams, frustrations, and yearning for something better. My verses became a bridge between two worlds—reconciling the ancient and the modern, the Mexican and the American, the poverty of our reality, and the boundless aspirations in our hearts.

Those writings became *Echoes of Aztlán*, the companion book you hold in your hands at this very moment—my journey told in verse. These poems attempt to capture the pain of displacement, the beauty of ancestral culture, and the enduring love found through hope that defines the immigrant experience. I invite you to walk alongside me—to see the world through my immigrant eyes, feel the struggles and triumphs of my story, and celebrate the resilience and humanity we all share.

Welcome to *Echoes of Aztlán*—a symphony of survival, a celebration of heritage, and a call to embrace the diverse threads that define our shared humanity.

CHAPTER 1
We Are Home on Our Land

On a hot, humid afternoon in the fields of Eastern Oregon, the air was filled with the sound of sprinklers watering a nearby crop. My family and I were busy hoeing weeds in a thirty-acre field. I was lagging, lost in thought, when I noticed a young boy riding a bicycle on the dirt road next to our field. He had a white towel flapping behind him, clamped to the back fender of his bike.

My imagination raced in multiple directions all at once, and it was difficult to realize where I was. As if time had stopped, I could feel the coolness of jumping into an aqua-blue pool completely submerged from reality. Maybe it was the suffocating humidity, stirred by the penetrating heat of the afternoon sun, which made me wonder: Was he headed to the local swimming pool? I wondered why this boy could enjoy the pool while I had to work in the fields. That summer day, I realized the unfairness of it all—that this boy was free to ride his bike to the pool while I worked under the relentless sun on his family's farm.

At the age of nine that summer in the Yakima Valley of Washington State, I began to question why kids my age had the freedom to ride their bikes, go swimming, and play in shaded parks filled with playgrounds while I spent my time in the fields. From that moment forward, I decided I would not live my life in the fields. As much as I loved and respected my family, I was determined that my life would be guided by the power of choice. I would find a better way to live, one that would allow me to go to the pool whenever I wanted.

The Impacts of Conquest

Mothers, fathers, brothers, sisters, bound by conquest,
blood mixes, cultures collide—
gods, ceremonies, rituals challenge the past,
ancient cities scatter.

Ancient wisdom, hidden, guarded, isolated—
exploitation resisted.
Civilizations abandoned, opal-shaped eyes gaze north.
Ancient spirits whisper, urging onward,
forging paths toward a future of migration and discovery.

Cities fall to ruin.
The human spirit embraces the natural world:
earth, water, wind, fire.
Land and water nourish a wandering people
seeking wisdom and new ways of being.

Assimilation births tribes of many colors:
black, brown, white—
languages merge, knowledge accumulates,
wisdom grows, vision evolves.
Expansion follows—ancient tribal lands rediscovered,
a return to origins: water, rivers, food, people.

From lands of whiteness, generations migrate north,
carrying science, art, and humanity,
sustaining the purity of land, water, and air.
Life and knowledge entwine as new cities rise,
souls of the past, spirits of the future,
await the dawn of a new millennium.

Modern cities built on ancient stones,
roads paved over ancient paths.
Old dreams revisited, we gather once more,
forming a new humanity of many colors.
The Aztec language is rediscovered
among the ruins of a forgotten world.

Timeworn community ceremonies
blend with modern habits.
The prophecy spoken in ancient tongues
speaks across the years to today.
Hidden knowledge manifests.
We have become a new people,
A new race of all.

The prophecy fulfilled—we are Raza!
We are home, on our land.

The Truth

Born an Aztec brave,
Warriors migrate to a new world—
A foreign language, food, and music,
A clash of cultures, gods, and nature.

In this new world, old ways are dismantled—
the Aztec sun has set,
the last of the original Indian sunsets.
Yet in the new sunrise is a birth of new ways.

New people, languages, art,
food, music, and culture emerge.
In the prophecy, the sunset prepares
the new millennium to welcome
new inhabitants.

The conquest begins.

I will never know the daylight of the ancients.
Generations have come and gone across Mother Earth.
Persecution, discrimination, and racism evolve,
sophisticated in how they are delivered by the conquerors.
Night has fallen for the last time on the Aztec way of life.

A new moon appears, ready to be born,
the invader's blood blends
with the Indian spirit as a new race rises.

When the sun goes down on this day,
it will never rise again as it was.
But the new day brings a new world
of mosques, temples, churches,
and science.

Under an Aztec Sun

I was born in a lettuce field,
shooting marbles in a labor camp,
dust thick on my breath.
As the eagle soared,
we traveled north in caravans,
sweat, salty and sweet,
lingering on my lips.
The earth cracked,
clenching the sweat from our bodies.
Our ancestors chased our shadows,
we worked a day's labor at twelve years of age.
Lost children laughing
in the fields and bodegas.

The Mexican Eagle

The eagle passes silently
over the valley of Mexico,
the journey's end from Aztlan,
our place of origin but a memory.

My spirit flew alongside the eagle,
wing tip to wing tip,
as you passed your knowledge.

You gave me the freedom to fly,
with love in my heart and your courage
to struggle with a pure heart.
The Aztec sun burned into my soul,

you taught me to believe in silent men—
voices screaming from their eyes.
You taught me the hope of a new culture,
history, pyramids, and faith
blended into the future.

I chased the eagle to new horizons,
perched at the dawn of history.

Pilgrims arrive in our world.
They build stick houses, drive bright-colored cars,
all over the land of Aztlán.

We speak in many tongues,
understanding one, hiding another,
all thirsty for the knowledge
of the unturned page.

You gave me friends in the forum,
the will to fly—
where the eagle passes to the north.

You gave me the chance to understand
why you love this new place,
a place that pushes back in resistance to our presence.

With your wisdom and love,
I have become a Mejicano of Aztlán.
I am Raza.

Sun of Life

Footsteps rise, echoes merging,
resounding down a long, shadowed hall.
A heartbeat draws nearer, pulsing, surging—
Excitement ripples, an ancient call.

Closer now to the Sun revered,
the source of life, of warmth, of fire.
through strife and channeling pathways clear,
each step is guided by the soul's desire.

Soon, the Sun of Life will be peaking,
its rays a promise, pure and true.
Drawn by a life of earnest seeking,
I walk, in spirit, toward the view.

Raza is Born

Vibrant sounds echo,
bounce from the forest floor,
reaching the canopy of trees.
Jungle wildlife erupts, tree to tree,
stretching toward the sky, a dream captured.
Aztec sun, serpent gods, night skies whisper
prophecies at the crossroads, pointing north
as foretold, the future will guide our path.
As we embark, a pyramid's shadow falls
on humid jungle paths, leading to a new world.
Forgotten symbols and languages, hidden in secrecy,
protecting the sacred knowledge from foreign invaders.
Indian wisdom is hidden from desecration.
Only the chosen people speak of the knowledge
in silence, hidden among the pyramids' stone walls.
The conquest brought men with hair-covered faces,
blue and green eyes, conquerors
mounted on beasts, carrying metal spears,
silver-bladed knives, swords, and exploding sticks.
The stars announced their coming.
Destruction without purpose. Without intent.
Lacking the understanding of consequence.
In transformation, time evolved through an earlier life,
bearing witness, waiting for the destiny of our children.
The path was chosen in a prophecy and repeated
in our stories over evening campfires.
Recollections of the genocidal invaders without honor.
Possessing a cultural rejection and intervening
in an ancient civilization.
Destruction!
Families torn apart, Indian blood flows,
daughters, sisters, mothers, forced into unions,
through alien collisions. New blood. New people.
Raza is born!

CHAPTER 2
Identity

I have noticed many young Mexican American children, like me, wrestle with endless identity struggles. To claim to be Mexican invites the stigma of being labeled "illegal," while calling oneself American can result in being dubbed "Tío Taco"—someone caught between two worlds with no clear path forward.

What is my true identity? Am I José or Joe? My parents call me José, but my teachers and peers renamed me Joe without my consent. I cannot recall when this transition occurred, but to me, it represents how my identity was often outside of my control.

Most children grow up learning playful nursery rhymes, but I cannot recall any from my childhood. I have often wondered how I could emerge into adulthood without those formative songs that seem so essential to other people's growth. I have met other Chicanos like me who never experienced the joy of those nursery rhymes in English or Spanish. We were children deprived of innocence, thrust into labor fields before we could grasp the tender embrace of our mothers. I have walked alongside Chicanos who, despite their deprived childhoods, possess a profound understanding of the world's demands and confront them with unshakable resolve. I am one of them, shaped by the challenges we face and the resilience we carry.

As the years passed without the luxury of childhood toys, dolls, or fairy tales, we found ourselves thrust into adulthood. The world demanded we compete as adults, yet we never experienced the innocence of childhood nor the privilege of defining ourselves as distinctly Mexican or American. Instead, we embraced the label Chicano—in defiance of the confusion.

To the outside world, it may seem enigmatic, but to us, it embodies a spirit, pride, and dignity. We wear Chicano as a badge of honor—a symbol of our unique identity—propelling us into leadership, yearning for recognition.

Raised to revere authority, we Mexican Americans were taught not to challenge it, fearing the consequences of defiance. Organizing, unionizing, or opposing the establishment was condemned by our elders as communist—a notion they fiercely rejected because they fought in World War II and the Korean War against socialists.

Mexico, our mother, turned her back on those who ventured north, offering no warm welcome, grieving the loss of her children. I longed to offer myself to the motherland, yet I was torn between two worlds imposed upon my spirit—belonging to neither. How could I discover myself when I remained adrift, unsure of where I truly belonged?

In the Beets

The early spring air is freshened by gentle rains,
it's time to plant; the beets are waiting—
their seeds readied to thrive in the rich, dark soil.
While the world sleeps, planting begins at dawn.
Farmworkers whisper prayers for a bountiful harvest
as the last remnants of snow melt away.
Early morning frost kisses their lips, purple and swollen.
They venture into the fields, hearts filled with thoughts of ancestors,
recalling the last harvest and the theft of their land and dignity.

Mint Field

Children play, their laughter ringing,
capturing their unrestrained, endless imagination.
Echoes of possibility ripple through the bodega—
it's time to prepare for the day's labor.
Men, women, and children awaken before dawn,
as the sun greets the eastern horizon,
and the earth slowly warms for its children's souls.
Together, they ready to clear thirty acres of weeds,
the youngest of children just learning to walk
wandering though the camp, too young to toil,
playing and resting under the shade of a tree,
a flatbed truck hidden among tall weeds
providing shelter from the scorching rays.
The cool, moist soil soothes aching fingers
as they penetrate the hardened crust of the earth.
Big-brimmed summer hats, baseball caps,
bandanas, and scarves shield the farmworkers
from the sun's torment as they march down the field.
A community lunch simmers over the campfire,
pinto beans waiting to quell midday hunger.
Chatter erupts as lunchtime approaches,
no topic is sacred—music, jokes, and infectious laughter
lift everyone's spirits as the aroma of food fills the air.
The lunch gathering swells with conversation,
concealed dreams, aspirations, and desires.
An elder guides a young farmworker—
"Grab a pair of leather gloves to protect your hands,"
he says, as the banquet concludes
in laughter and hope.
"Forget the soft brown cotton gloves;
leather will protect you. Sharpen your hoe;
make it easier on yourself."
In the distance, small figures march to the mint field,
a battalion of farmworkers on a mission to conquer,

methodically eliminating every weed,
their heads adorned with vibrant reds, blues, and browns
each hat and bandana respectful of the Aztec sun,
which offers no mercy.
Moments pass, and sweat dries, leaving salty stains
on loosely fitted clothing. Clearing the thirty acres
is the objective of the day. Heat waves rise into the afternoon,
distant conversations blending with ancestral chants,
a prayer to the Sun God—
"Be merciful on those harvesting your bounty."
Songs and laughter fill the afternoon air.
And tomorrow, we will do this again;
we harvest so they can eat.

Born in the Beets

When autumn whispers at winter's door,
with the first frost, a fog settles over waiting fields.
Farmworkers arrive, preparing for their migration,
a time of harvest approaches, stable homes transferred
to labor camps—temporary shelters—
a migrant child's playground among rows of sprouting beets,
where dark, moist soil cradles dreams.
I was born in the beets, grew up with the scent of mint, alfalfa,
and livestock.
Through spring, summer, and fall, harvest is the reward.
Families travel with the soaring eagle to the north,
returning to their origins where rituals of antiquity beckon.
A journey of livelihood, working today for tomorrow's promise,
A necessary patience to endure, waiting through winter's grasp.
When harvest time arrives, they travel in caravans,
families from the colonia transported along the interstate,
chasing the sunset, trucks laden with belongings,
water bags filled, food prepared, stocked for what may come.
Laughter erupts, family humor lifting the weight of stress.
Salad bowl crops await the touch of humanity,
ready to be taken from their birthplace to nourish others.
Moist ground dries into a talcum powder of dust,
blowing easily into unprotected eyes; calloused hands penetrate
the protective shell, breaking the earth, dust erupts,
attacking intruders, as sacred food is disturbed; beets resist,
fighting against separation from the gods' nourishment.
By midday, sweat rounds their lips, earth cracked by heat,
absorbing the moisture from weary bodies.
At the weekend dance, Sunday families gather,
the promised return trip home giving them strength to
continue.

Eagles Pass

Forced by conflict to abandon their ancestral dwellings,
we learned to imagine what could be with hearts filled with hope.
We looked to the horizon, to the eagle's flight, searching for
the courage to struggle in a fight belonging to all.
Ancestors taught us how to believe, how to dream
In silence, we bear a silent strength,
Proclaiming pride in our origins while embracing new cultures,
creating new histories, merging races,
we built modern
pyramids.
Our faith in the past intertwined with prophecies for the
future—we chased the eagle to new horizons, a new civilization.
Like ancient pilgrims arriving at new lands,
Waiting to observe the eagles perching at the dawn of history.
Hailing from every corner of Aztlán,
we absorb the unknown, speaking in diverse tongues,
understanding one another, thirsting to know all,
willing to forge a new history, to be made, to be re-made.
Unaware of the unturned pages ahead and behind,
we believed and found friendship through differences,
given the will to fly where the eagle passed.
Ancestors planting seeds of ancient crops in new fields,
our will to pursue the journey north was a chance to become.

Mestizo

As foretold, a Mestizo is born,
destined for eternity, shaped by ancient prophecy.
A civilization transforms under the conquest of foreign invaders—
red hair, blue eyes, an unknown tongue, rituals on their knees,
religious symbols depicting the four destructions,
as foretold by elders and Aztec priests.
Forever! Change, chaos, turmoil, oppression, captive lives.
Red eyes in the dark of night glow like hot coals.
Raging pain surges as families shatter—
divided, mothers, wives, sisters, taken.
Mixed lineage emerges, secrets weave into existence.
Invaders claim the forbidden; children are raised in two worlds.
Rebellion ignites, resistance inspires!
A new world forms, heartbeats pound,
sounds of crying children pierce the silent sky.
Streams of Indian tears overflow, pushed downward,
rose-colored cheeks dampened by deep sorrow.
Voices clash in defiance, breaking the silence—
a black mirrored night shattering into stardust.
A Mestizo child is born in conflict and resistance.

Hermiston

Yesterday, we posed like sculpted statues.
A humble, proud dreamer stood alone amidst the throng,
hypnotized by long golden hair, curled to perfection,
entranced by youthful imagination, light bulbs flash, smiles sparkle,
laughter erupted as we disassembled, drifting apart.
The young Cub Scout dared to explore his racing fantasies,
reserved for grown men, rarely bestowed upon young love.
Would she notice the blue suit of armor?
Together in the picture, they discovered each other,
posed like statues, they revealed the daydream.
A golden chain encircled the young man's neck,
binding faith to the infinite future,
changing a young life, ever-present—
a recollection of a single moment,
tickets for final destinations
already purchased, final paths selected.

Chicano Education

Silent bodies sit motionless, protesting without bloodshed,
awaiting commands, directions to follow, stop, or lead.
Our naïve, innocent eyes cannot pierce the professor's heart.

The professor repeats instructions and meaningless commands—
lectures on what was, what might be, all go unquestioned,
reverberating throughout ivory towers.
One student speaks—dares to raise a hand,

but the professor's lips slap together, cracking against pale skin.
Incomprehensible, there will be no questions!
The pointer drifts across the slate,
adrift in a meaningless, pale green sea of knowledge.

Marble hallways hide secrets of assimilation,
questions sprout in a fertile garden, yet have no vehicle for expression,
silent meditation brews, rebellion simmers.
Like inscriptions on a stone wall guided by the past,
next week's assignment is etched on the board.

Ah! Mission accomplished!
The handcrafted sterilization of people
one color, one class.
People of color, the poor, women—omitted!

Children

The sun glares in the midafternoon brightness,
heating Mother Earth. Eggs fry on sidewalks,
blinding crystals spark from solar reflections,
a nearby lake shares mirrored images of everything.
Aqua-colored waters resembling gulf waters reflect Tulum.
Throughout the day, children play like pyramid silhouettes in the backyard.
The children of antiquity dance between the known and the unknown future,
Siblings of what was and what will be: mother, father, friend,
Three points of the pyramid. Can't you see the sun beginning to set?
The darkness opens the door, creeping further west.
It will be a long dark night; they hold each other until dawn,
as children awaken to the new Aztec sun of the Yucatan,
they are greeted. What will become of the children?

The Crying Lady (La Llorona)

My uncle's eyes were wide enough to reflect my image,
a skull tattoo was etched on his right forearm,
with a dagger piercing through, dripping teardrop blood.

"¿Qué pasa, Tío?" I asked.

He said nothing, but I felt fear waiting,
endless time, no beginning, no end, just now, no answer.

"I need to know, are the cops coming?"
He hit someone, the thought raced through my mind.
Like that flashy '57 Chevy! Uncle!
Was it a fight? A gun or knife?

Waiting like an anxious patient, his eyes unblinking, wide open,
still waiting, his body flash-frozen, motionless,
"I saw her," he blurted out, "¡La Llorona!" She is real!

La Llorona, a campfire story told by the old folks,
Is she a story retold, dream or real?
A weeping woman wandering the roadsides,
riverbanks, isolated dark corners of our minds.
Searching for the lost children of Mexico.
A campfire tale scaring children into bed,
La Llorona seeded in young minds,
ready to sprout succeeding into adult minds.

"¿Qué pasó, Tío?" I asked.

"She was there on the side of the road."

"Doing what?"

"Searching," like the old folks say.

"It's just a campfire story, La Llorona."

I wondered—was my uncle lost? Was he a threat? Did he cause harm?
Who was she protecting?
He was the one
driving drunk at 2 AM, teetering on the edge of danger.
She was there in a flowing white gown,
veil covering her face. She bolted toward the car—
my uncle screamed in fear!

Stepping on the gas, he sped away,
But she floated alongside the car, no matter the speed
Scratching the side panel, reaching for him.

"I will never drink again!"

Not convinced, at sunrise, I examined the car,
finding scratch marks the length of the vehicle,
from the headlight to the back fender,
to the end of the car.

La Llorona continues to search
for her lost children of Mexico.

CHAPTER 3
The Uncle Factor

At nineteen years old, my father joined the Army during World War II and deployed to the Pacific, where he served through the long years of war. A generation later, in 1969, when I turned eighteen, I volunteered to serve as well, unaware that I was following his path more closely than I realized. Processing into the military at Fort Lewis, Washington, I was walking in my father's footsteps, retracing a journey he had taken twenty-six years earlier.

I can still see those long lines of young men from all over the country, all waiting for haircuts, uniforms, boots, and the gear that would make us soldiers. One afternoon, as I was standing in one of those long lines, I leaned against an old wooden beam that supported one of those aging World War II buildings. As I stood there, waiting for my turn, I absentmindedly began reading the names carved into the wood. And then I froze. A chill crept from the top of my head down to the back of my neck as I read a name: Victor E. Vasquez. My father's name. Could it be the same Victor E. Vasquez standing in this very spot years before me? How many men with that name could have passed through here?

My legs almost gave way. In that moment, I realized I was standing where my father had once stood, in a place where he had carved his name, leaving a part of himself behind. A wave of sadness and pride filled my heart. I began to understand his silence, the weight he had carried, and the quiet sincerity in his eyes.

It was weeks before I could finally call him. When I did, with a mix of excitement and reverence, I asked, "Dad, do you remember carving your name on a beam at Fort Lewis?" There was a pause on the other end of the line, then he said softly, "Yes, mijo. I carved my name at every place I was stationed." His answer hit me like a wave. I realized then that I was not just following in his footsteps but honoring a tradition, one that ran through our family like a steady current.

Since that day, I have carried a deep sense of pride, knowing I stood where my father, uncles, and cousins once stood. In our family, serving in the military was not about the glory of battle; it was about giving back and a shared sense of duty to our country and one another. For me, it was not about becoming a warrior but continuing a legacy built on sacrifice and service.

As I reflected more, I came to see my decision to enlist as a natural part of what I came to learn was the "Uncle Factor." Growing up, my willingness to serve was shaped by the example set by the men in my family—my father, my uncles, my cousins—all of whom had worn the uniform with quiet dignity. In our home, walking into the living room meant seeing certain things on the wall: a picture of La Virgen de Guadalupe, a portrait of President Kennedy, and photos of family members proudly wearing their military uniforms. These images were not just decorations; they were symbols of faith, pride, and sacrifice. They reminded us of what it meant to be patriota in our community.

I absorbed the lessons of service and duty, not through words but through actions, through the unspoken legacy of those I admired. I learned that being a patriot wasn't about waving a flag; it was about standing up for something larger than yourself, something rooted in the sacrifices of those who came before. And so, I served—not to seek glory, but to honor a legacy, to give back to those who had given so much to me.

Looking back now, I see my father and uncles as the true patriots whose quiet acts of service shaped my understanding of duty, sacrifice, and resilience. Dios bendiga the young men and women, and their families, who have given so much, just as my family did. The legacy of service is a sacred thread, binding generations, each one adding their own chapter to a story of love, pride, and unyielding strength. Que siempre viva su memoria, their stories etched into our hearts and in the places we once stood together.

In the barrios and colonias across the country, young Latino men and women lived lives marked by both dreams and hardships. Many were the children of migrant farm workers, laboring alongside their families under the unforgiving sun, harvesting crops in fields that never seemed to yield enough. Their families, holding tight to the promise of a better future, often faced deep economic challenges and limited opportunities. For these young Latinos, the allure of a stable job through military service seemed like a beacon of hope, a way to break free from the cycle of poverty and create a brighter path for themselves and their loved ones.

At eighteen, grappling with such complexities is difficult, especially when faced with the prospect of fighting for a country that once invaded and fought against our ancestral homeland. Yet, pride persists—fueled by the extraordinary courage to serve a nation that bestows countless derogatory epithets on us, names we bear because of being stripped of status and dignity. And still, at eighteen, our anger was set aside to serve.

Back home, the impact of the war rippled through Latino communities like a slow, painful wave. Families who had sent their sons and daughters to fight in a war not of their making were left in a state of uncertainty and grief. The pillars of these families, the primary breadwinners, were either lost in the war or returned unable to work. The government's promises—of benefits, opportunities, and a better life—too often fell short. Disillusionment settled in as veterans struggled to find their place in a society that had made them invisible.

Yet even in the face of these deep challenges, the resilience of Latino communities shone through. Families banded together, drawing on their shared cultural strength and traditions of solidarity. Grassroots movements and advocacy groups emerged, fighting tirelessly for the rights of Latino veterans and their families. Organizations like the American GI Forum became champions for nuestros veteranos, ensuring they received the recognition and support they deserved. The war, while a period of immense suffering, also sparked the broader Movimiento Chicano. Latinos nationwide began to demand civil rights, better education, and economic opportunities, fueled by the shared sense that their sacrifices must not go unnoticed.

The Vietnam War, while devastating, ignited a spirit of activism and change within Latino communities. Nuestra gente came together, drawing strength from their cultural heritage and the stories passed down from their abuelos and ancestors. They fought not just for themselves but for a more just and equitable society for all marginalized groups. The war, in all its pain, had given birth to a new fight—a fight for dignity, for justice, for la comunidad.

In the end, the story of the Vietnam War's impact on poor Americans—especially Latinos—is one of both profound sorrow and remarkable perseverance. It is a testament to the enduring spirit of a people whose quest for dignity and justice continues, even in the face of overwhelming adversity. For me, the story is personal. It is the story of my family, of my father and uncles—what we often call the "Uncle Factor"—their influence leading me to a life of service. Like so many others, our stories are tied to the legacy of this war and the larger, unending fight for nuestro lugar in this country.

American Aztec Warriors

Warriors' hands dig deep in the earth,
farmworker-warriors planting to feed
a miracle in waiting, seeds ready to grow,
destined to nourish millions. While others sleep,
the warriors' plant, praying for rain,
asking the earth to accept their offering.
"Let them survive," they whisper.

A shiver breaks, piercing cold chills,
still, they march onto the field to harvest,
faces red from the cold, lips chapped,
hearts strong with purpose, they serve.
Sunset signaling their day's end, dinner at last,
chewing on week-old tortillas, food long gone.
Asking for a raise would be rude.

In the quiet, they remember ancestral warriors,
who had their dignity stolen, but their legacy reborn.
In the beet fields, modern warriors toil.
Around campfires, knowledge is preserved,
Stories of ancient battles retold.
We were born warriors—silent, proud,
And now, the warrior's hall waits for the beet harvest to end.

Orders

Warriors come from across the country,
patriots of every color, every corner of the world,
months of preparation leading them here—
to meet their fate, united in common purpose.
Waiting for the next duty station,
their orders unknown, their leaders unseen,
they wait with the patience of monks,
silent prayers turning to hours, then days.
Twelve hundred soldiers stand in formation,
dressed in pickle-green, waiting.
Five hours pass, same line, same spot.
Eight hours bring heat and humid frustration.
Twelve hours in that frozen line,
rebellion creeps into disciplined minds.
From sunrise to sunset, no orders, no movement,
just the knowledge that none have arrived—
not today, not yet.
At last, a pickle suit with silver bars,
the symbol of authority, surely, he will know.
But as the crimson sunset fades,
He, too, brings unanswered questions.
Finally, patient warriors receive their orders—
time to dine,
a meal prepared by nineteen-year-old chefs.
Twelve hundred anxious, angry men accept their fate.
No orders for tomorrow, only the end of another day.
Marching in formation,
retreating to the old WWII barracks,
they count their blessings.
No orders yet.
As silence falls over the camp,
a blue moon breaks through the clouds.
Five thousand new pickle suits arrive tomorrow.
Where have they been?

Another day ends without a destination,
without answers.
Lying in the quiet, midnight passes.
One am, two am, without announcement, a song begins.
From the barracks, an unknown soldier sings,
"Summertime, and the livin' is easy."
The melody bounces off the white-painted walls,
echoing across the camp.
In that moment, I understood:
The orders we await do not matter.
Our path is already mapped,
our fate, already drawn.

Mexican American Veteran

Vietnam brought us home once and for all. In the same dream we all march in unison: low-rider trucks, bumper stickers decked out with the red, white, and blue. 'We're proud to be American,' we chant. But always somewhere a lesson yet to learn, a longing to belong, and never to forget we've paid the price with blood.
~ Chicano poet and writer Tino Villanueva, from his poem "I Have Walked the Rio Grande."

Young warriors assemble around an infinite circle,
as a timeless campfire burns—blue and orange flames blaze,
dancing shadows flicker across brown, weathered faces,
chiseled, ancient features—Indigenous faces smile,
laughter breaks, stories of the day's battles whispered,
fires burn uncontrolled,
flames exposing the soles of their worn sandals,
and the turmoil buried deep within.
Shadows of their ancestors dance on the angry flames,
Aztec power rising in the heat, a ceremonial dance,
like the warriors who came before,
preparing for battles yet to come.
Not with swords, but with guns. The survival of assimilation.
The sweet scent of burning leather mingles
with the locust wood, stoking the fire,
echoes of ancient songs swirl in the smoke,
bursting through the sound of young men
cracking open another beer,
laughter breaking through the reality of near-death.
"Hey loco, get me another beer," one calls,

another warrior's tale ready to be told.
The sound of distant cars rushing nowhere fills the night,
highways foreign to the hands that built them—
once migrant farmworkers, now displaced warriors,
those highways lead to homes they'll never own—
open-beamed ceilings, skylights, and pools beyond reach,
a gated entrance, no code to enter.
"For sale," the flyer reads,
"$0 down, FHA/VA approved. Why rent, Migrant?"
The fire burns brighter as an elder speaks in a forgotten tongue.
The warriors fall silent, setting down their beers,
listening to the prophecy of reclaiming stolen lands,
his calloused hands and sun-wrinkled face tell stories
of cornfields a thousand years old—
the migration north, highways paved over the path to Aztlán.
Your dream home, covered beneath the Aztec Sun.

Boy Soldiers

High school dreams of fast cars and fleeting loves,
cruising Main Street, Southern Comfort in paper cups,
dark nights lit by brilliant stars, the glorious moon guiding the way.
Wolfman Jack's voice howls through the radio,
rock and roll shaking the world.
squealing tires chase after pretty girls on the gut.
Along the riverbank, obsidian hair whips in the soft desert wind,
a full moon smothering the actions of reckless youth.
Dreams of "the one" fill their minds,
painful, everlasting passions—they wonder, when will they arrive?
Weekend keggers by the river's edge,
campfires crackle in the peace of starlit nights,
music explodes, sparks of what could be reflected in the river's glossy back,
eyes sparkling, heartbeats racing—
reflections of a full moon dance across the water,
stories whispered between songs—
tomorrow creeps closer with the sunrise teasing the night.
"What will you be when you grow up?" someone asks.
"I don't know, I don't care," is the answer.
The world feels endless until silence breaks like shattered glass.
Main streetlights flash yellow and red—
warnings ignored by immortal youth,
living in moments untouched by time,
until reality interrupts, bleeding through the evening news.
Parents sit in silence, smoking cigarettes,
kill ratios interrupt dinner conversations,
prayers whispered in solitude,
brothers and sisters arguing over the dishes.
Monday arrives—reality intrudes,
classrooms filled with smiling faces hiding faint thoughts.
"What does the war mean to us"? "What is freedom?

Why are we asked to go? Where will we go?"
Reckless as colts, their youth trembles on shaky legs,
who will go first?
Chaos chases them, forcing maturity far too soon.
Plans form in young men's minds,
visions of a near future scrawled on bathroom walls,
weekend dances filled with dreams of stolen kisses,
solitude in the quiet—yesterday has become today.
Tomorrow interrupts everything.
A reckless caress, a virgin kiss,
youth interrupted, missing the depth of intimate love.
A child's voyage cut short, the end drawing near.
Young men awaken to a modern reality—
Is it a conflict or a war?
Eighteen, and now what?
Graduation arrives—spring brings cool rains,
family celebrations and weekend parties filled with uncertainty.
The trees sprout leaves, heat waves rise—
and the first draft letter arrives.
To be safe or to be destroyed?
The invitation comes—
a physical exam, foreign lands, foreign people, foreign loves.
Fear creeps in—
A door opens, and the choice is made,
or perhaps the choice was made for them.
A greeting from Uncle Sam,
only nineteen years old—
dear God, why me?

Sunset

Is it the beginning or the end of education—
a grade school with Sunset as a name.
a gathering place for education,
where learning from each other was taught.
We arrived ready to play, to live, to discover.
Our first day, we were blank slates—
not knowing a soul, void of life lessons.
Life itself was a fleeting notion,
a moment with no past or future,
where only the last joke mattered.
Joy was the cluttered playground we called our own,
territory to claim, friendships to be found.
John, the bookworm, was the first to join the circle,
arriving with a book in hand, inquisitive, heart wide open.
Rick followed—a whirlwind of energy, laughter, and mischief.
And then came Rocky, a partner-in-crime,
together, they sparked a rebellion in play.
Then Greg arrived—serious, stable,
Finally, I was there, silently observing,
waiting to see where we would all end up,
a calming presence to our unpredictable storm.
Laughter swelled as the bonds grew stronger,
unconditional, chaotic, but full of meaning.
A brotherhood was formed, a lasting bond
that grew from the playground of Sunset
to the adolescent halls of high school.
Then—our country needed boys—
boys with no purpose, no direction,
poor and willing, perfect targets for Uncle Sam's call.
I was the first.
The Boys of Sunset were lottery winners that cold December,
and we unlearned all that was good.
Filled with conflict, fear, and hope all at once,
off we went, unprepared but fearless.

Time passed, and I returned—
But the Boys of Sunset did not.
John, lost to Agent Orange.
Rick and his dog, taken by the Texas Rangers,
in a shoot-out on a street in Dallas.
Robert, gunned down while robbing a gas station.
Greg, MIA in the jungles of Vietnam.
The Boys of Sunset taught me the meaning of brotherhood,
a love forged in laughter and lost in war.

Greyhound

A young warrior boards a blue, red, gray chariot,
a Greyhound ready to take him toward an unknown adventure,
while a televised battle plays in his mind.
The rhythm of rock and roll hums a prayer:
"War, what is it good for?"
Sweethearts left behind,
love that was now slipping away—
the love that could have been,
now just another casualty of time.
Not ready, the warrior boards the chariot,
fear and rage grip his gut, twisting into a knot.
Silent screams echo—Why? Why him? Why now?
The would-be warrior seeks another way,
hoping for peace, a soldier in a boy's body,
preparing to embrace the mystery of what's to come.
Staring out the rectangle window of the Greyhound bus,
a window into the future,
knowing that to have life and love
means losing everything that is cherished.
Relinquishing, he decides—if I have nothing,
I lose nothing.
Empty now,
he stares through the fogged-up glass,
carefully clearing a small circle,
spying on his family as the chariot begins to roll.
The high school sweetheart he should marry,
fading like the fog creeping onto the road ahead.
Fear and rage burst into a small cry,
the child within peeks into the future
through the eyes of a warrior.
I'm only 19 years old. I don't want to die.
Where is Vietnam? Who says this is important?
Facing the unknown,
he finds unfamiliar companions:

Fear.
Rage.
But God will be his guardian.

A Young Man Off to War

Eighteen years old—
a young man, or still just a boy?
Receives an official-looking letter
stamped with the mark of the Selective Service System.
"Order to Report for Induction."
Induction? What does it mean?
Who will I report to?
What will they do to me?

It's the first journey away from home,
to an unknown city,
to stand before men in uniform—
Army, Marines, all staring down at boys
barely old enough to shave.
A room full of hearts, brave and pure,
each one leaving behind a life,
a mother, a sweetheart, a home.
One hundred and fifty boys,
almost men,
lined up in their Fruit of the Looms,
facing each other.
"Drop your drawers!"
The command turns boys into sheep,
exposing more than skin—
a glimpse into the unknown.
Doctors in uniforms,
Inspect these young bodies,
one by one.

The daylong series of examinations ends,
and still, they ask—what's next?
They march into a room with red carpeting,
American flags standing tall like sentinels,
a podium guarding a temple of patriotism.

They are asked to swear an oath,
to make the ultimate sacrifice,
for a land far away,
for reasons they barely understand.
They are trained,
prepared to commit acts that conflict with their souls,
their beliefs are in tatters.

They march for miles,
through fields and dust-choked roads,
minds filled with thoughts of home,
of those left behind.
Days blur into weeks,
and hopelessness begins to creep in,
unraveling the steel they were told to forge.
In the darkness of night,
the questions come—
What is right?
What is just?

Their time arrives—
they are sent to unknown places,
scattered across the world.
Back home, families huddle by the evening news,
watching the names scroll across the screen,
scanning for brothers, sisters, aunts, uncles, friends,
wondering, praying,
as the number of fallen climbs.

Conflicted

In a neighborhood of only poverty, we learn to read and write on walls and streets. We struggle against a system that does not want us. We are the unwanted ones, yet we dream and learn in our own ways.

~ Chicano poet and activist Luis J. Rodriguez, from his poem "The Concrete River "

A young man stands, fists clenched in anger,
screams all around him, yet no one hears—
the violence, the noise, the confusion.
His heart, caught in the struggle,
torn by the paradox of his existence.

Gone are the days of dust in his eyes,
a hoe in hand, working the earth.
The future is no longer his to shape—
it has been decided by the weight of the past.

His soul drifts, caught between the lands of his ancestors,
where corn was once harvested and wisdom gathered.
Now, in a new world, he finds himself,
pitted against his own spirit.
Who am I? Where did I come from?
Indian, Mexican, or American?
I am Chicano!

Resistance

Caught! Society's iron fist tightens,
squeezing the spirit's last breath of resistance.
Arms crossed, muscles tense,
fighting against the unseen chains.
Exhausted, yet refusing to yield,
I wrestle with whispers—
"Give up, it will be easier."
Temptation pulls at my soul,
beckoning me toward what's comfortable,
but I refuse to be seduced by the unknown,
by false promises in trade for submission.
Demanding that I stop searching for the truth,
society pushes, pulls, and yanks—
every breath I take with lungs exhausted,
threatens to suffocate me.
Only rebellion remains.
My mind, like a coiled snake,
strikes back,
lashing out in a final attempt to be free.
I attack the enemy—
he stands in polished patent leather shoes,
his reflection staring back at me
through a glossy leather mirror.
Fear becomes my shadow.
He knows he has given his spirit
to cold cement monasteries
He is trying to steal mine. Yet I hold firm.
I will stay true to my soul.

CHAPTER 4
Formula for Rebellion

In the early 1960s, my family lived in a close-knit Mexican American neighborhood called a "Colonia" in Eagle Pass, Texas. Our home was modest, and we spoke Spanish at home, reserving English for school and the outside world. The air was always filled with the rich aromas of my aunt's cooking—tamales, enchiladas, and fresh tortillas.

My neighborhood was a vibrant mosaic of life. Families gathered in local parks for picnics on weekends, playing norteña or mariachi music on portable radios. The Colonia kids played soccer in the streets while our abuelitas sat on porches, chatting, and keeping a watchful eye on us. The community was a sanctuary of shared culture and mutual support.

When I first started school, I encountered a vastly different world. My elementary school was predominantly White, and the curriculum was heavily Anglicized. Speaking Spanish was discouraged—sometimes even punished. I struggled with the duality of my identity, feeling the pressure to assimilate at school while cherishing my Mexican heritage at home.

By the time I was in junior high, I began to see more clearly the inequalities my community faced. Our textbooks seemed outdated, with no mention of Mexican Americans' contributions to U.S. history. The schools on the poorer side of town, where I lived, were noticeably more run-down compared to those on the wealthier side. These disparities planted the seeds of awareness and a desire for change in me.

When I entered high school in the late 1960s, the Chicano Movement was gaining momentum. Leaders like César Chávez, who was organizing farmworkers for better conditions, and events like the Chicano Moratorium, which protested the Vietnam War's impact on Mexican American youth, inspired me with a sense of pride and purpose.

While still in high school, I joined student groups fighting for better housing and wages for farmworkers, bilingual education, and improved school facilities. The iconic "Walkouts" of 1968, where thousands of students left their classrooms to demand educational reform, was a turning point for me.

Despite the turbulence of those times, my family remained a cornerstone of my life. Sunday dinners were sacred—usually a barbecue of cabrito or fajitas. These mealtimes were filled with laughter, stories, and the comfort of tradition. My aunts and uncles shared tales of their own struggles and triumphs, grounding me with a deep sense of Indigenous history and resilience.

Celebrations like quinceañeras, weddings, and Día de los Muertos were vital threads in the fabric of my community life. These events reinforced my connection to my roots and provided a strong counterbalance to the external pressures of assimilation.

Assimilation

Two souls exchange consciousness,
an awareness of each other
that eternity cannot take away.
A song from hell shrieks,
echoing, vibrating, tremors of struggle.
The transparency of thought—
simulated motions of acceptance,
explosive rhetoric demanding change.
a notion of creating an equitable society,
a futuristic optimism of institutional reform.
Yet, at birth, condemned to the acid of failure,
we try to build this new world through CHANGE.
Yet artificial nature forbids the colors to blend,
without amputating the malignant limb,
The infection of hatred will spread unchecked.
The tune of the song is different,
but the words are the same.
Change the song—
accept the need to change
both the tune and the words.

Remember the Revolution

Remember the Revolution?
Brother! Sister!
It was three movies and two new cars ago,
back when I was still full of life—Alive!
Yeah, remember?
We were alive with anger, tears in our eyes,
chasing dreams of justice for all our brothers and sisters.
Dreams of being treated like human beings.
Oh, how it could have been.
Remember the Revolution?
Brother, where have we gone?
Into a world that cheated our families of love,
where once I dwelled on the thought of injustice,
with anger in my voice, I condemned the institutions,
chasing dreams of a world without structure—
grasping at chaos, trying to redefine everything.
I refused to participate in a world
that gave me luxury while wearing a uniform of shame.
I beat my head against artificial walls of paper,
books of Western civilization
open vision to the past
with centuries behind them.
My realization! It was a gift,
opening a vision of the past,
preparing for the future
given only to those who live here.
Harvard—an institution, once out of reach
for the son of a migrant worker,
a testimony to what's possible,
even for those like me. Who once hated.
An institution for the mind—
a place to provoke, rebel, and debate—
it opened its doors
to those who wish to make a better world.

The doors were opened to me—
Brother, where have we gone?

Pipeline

A pipeline needs to be built.
Coldfoot, one of twelve camps—
pump stations serving as launching pads
for hundreds of miles across mountains.

Eight hundred rudderless workers in one camp,
each waiting to create a story,
captured by wanderlust, seeking extraordinary adventure.

A combined curiosity peaks; the arrival begins.
A frozen runway awaits,
snow-covered mountains surround
the temporary wooden shells,
trailers serving as home for the transient.
Nature's challenge of unforgivable control,
a forbidden will to challenge a natural power,
the mother herself stands up to the confrontation—
the Arctic Circle is the fighter's ring
where Mother Earth will combat the invaders,
challengers to nature.

A ridiculous arrogance driving construction
an atrocity to the natural way of life itself.
We are committing sinful acts against Mother Nature,
a world not meant for a pipeline.

Unnatural construction designed to feed a society
with a need for endless consumption.
Thirty below in spring—
it is not winter; how much daylight do we have?
How cold will it get in the winter?

Urgency creeps in, a need to revel in the light of day.
As the days grow longer, the madness of a cold, dark winter
fades.

Three winters have passed, living with the madness—
endless nights exploring, learning more of who I am,
where I stand.

I will walk away with a relationship to the Earth Mother;
awareness arrives unsolicited—I am a small piece of the universe,
guided by a greater spiritual power of the rainbow lights,
Indigenous peoples dancing across the sky playing
games while hidden in the northern lights.

Nature will outlast the wounds we inflict;
the great pipeline will only be temporary.
We will fade into the fabric of a natural cycle.

Coldfoot Winter

Coldfoot Camp was one of thirty-one Trans Alaska Pipeline
construction camps located north of Fairbanks within the Arctic
Circle in the middle of Brooks Range.

Months of darkness fade,
a three-minute sunrise followed by sunset.
darkness resists the light,
each sunrise measured by the minute.

Solitude has been my only companion,
three months pass, endless darkness, daylight in wait—
absent of shadows, invisible spirits dance freely,
not being noticed; equilibrium compromised.

Individual senses of direction fade,
external stimulation is limited by a blanket of whiteness.
The northern earth illuminates under the stars,
as the northern lights dance across the horizon.

A three-minute sunrise announces a new arrival—
the pending arrival of missing daytime shadows.
Finally! Others may soon arrive—new voices, new faces.
Ah, conversation! My memory records the voices
of eleven construction workers who braved
darkness during the Alaska winter.

Twelve endured winter's torment, nature's confinement.
Time extends, and the sun's light lingers longer,
a few minutes each day; anticipation seeds anxiety—
knowing that others will arrive soon.

Will we? The isolated twelve know how to converse.
Will too many people arrive?
Twelve in camp was too little.
Will eight hundred souls be too many?

Eight hundred people will arrive in a week—
a population explosion!
Daylight arrives, the weather clears,
planes begin to land—three planes a day.

CHAPTER 5
Thoughts of Love

The volatility of my upbringing taught me to be sensitive to the delicate threads of human connection. I lived in numerous small rural communities, traveling with family as migrant farmworkers to many picturesque settings surrounded by rolling hills with snow-covered mountains and forests in the distance. The second oldest of my aunts, Guadalupe (Lupe), was known for her kindness and how her laughter could light up even the darkest corners of our cabins. Yet, despite her joyful nature, she harbored a secret longing within her heart—a quest for love. Throughout her life, she remained single, always taking care of the family first—and kids like me who had no mother and depended on my dad, aunts, and uncles.

Lupe told me she often pondered the nature of love as she wandered, working in the fields during the day and caring for the children in the evening. Alone in her thoughts was a woven tapestry of thoughts, hopes, and dreams about what love might and could be. She watched as couples strolled hand in hand, their faces glowing with a quiet contentment that seemed almost otherworldly.

"What is love built on?" she mused aloud one evening, her voice barely a whisper against the setting sun.

Lupe's grandmother, who had raised her after her parents had passed away, listened intently. "Love is not something you can seek or find, dear one," she gently answered. "It cannot be chosen or picked like a flower from the meadow. Love is something deeper, something that inspires and challenges you."

According to my aunt Lupe, her grandmother spoke of love

as if it were a living, breathing entity, unpredictable and wild. "Love is not for the timid or the weak," she continued. "It cannot be planned or controlled. It is a gift, given freely, and it demands as much as it gives."

Intrigued, Lupe began to see love not as a destination but as a journey, a path that could only be walked with faith and hope. She realized that love required belief—not just in the other person, but in the possibility of love itself. It was a force that could strengthen the soul and bring joy to the spirit, a force that could confuse and inspire in equal measure.

As days turned into months, Lupe's understanding of love deepened and was passed on to me. She saw it in the way her grandmother's eyes sparkled when she recounted stories of her own youthful romance. She felt it in the warmth of a friend's embrace and heard it in the laughter shared over simple pleasures. Love, she discovered, was not always grand declarations or dramatic gestures. Often, it was in the unspoken belief and trust between two people, in the small moments that wove their lives together.

One crisp autumn day, as the leaves turned to hues of gold and crimson, Lupe met a young man named Alberto. He was a wanderer, a soul as free and untamed as the wind. Their paths crossed by chance or fate in one of the labor camps. Alberto's spirit mirrored her own—full of dreams yet grounded in a deep sense of wonder.

There was a spark between Lupe and Alberto from their first meeting, an unspoken connection that words could never fully capture. They walked together, talked for hours, and found solace in each other's company. Love, as her grandmother had said, was not something they chose; it simply blossomed, unbidden and pure.

Lupe and Alberto's love was not without its challenges. There were moments of doubt and times when the road seemed uncertain. But through it all, their love remained a constant, an unyielding force that bound them together. It demanded their courage, their faith, and their hope. It was a love that was given freely, without reservation, and it brought them a joy that neither had ever known.

Hand in hand, side by side, Lupe and Alberto faced the world together. Their love became a beacon, a testament to the belief that love is not something you can control or plan. It is a strength to the soul, a joy to the spirit, and a promise of eternal life together.

In the end, Lupe understood that her quest for love had not been a journey to find something external. Instead, it was a journey of the heart, a quest to open herself to the possibility of love, to believe in its power, and to let it inspire and transform her. And as she stood beside Alberto, watching the sun set over the hills, she knew that her love was not just a fleeting feeling but a profound, unspoken belief in each other—a belief that would carry them through the days and years to come. Lupe knew she had found what love is truly built on.

What I learned from listening to my Tía Lupe recount her memories was that I must look within to learn about myself. I could not intentionally seek love while holding a prescribed notion of what I believed love should be. Lupe constantly reinforced the idea that I could not look for love like I was buying a new car. Love is not something to be examined or tested to see how it drives. People get consumed in the quest for love with an uncontrollable fervor, but it cannot be chosen. For some, it becomes a journey that can take years, sometimes decades, to realize. Like Lupe, I searched for the elusive notion of love, a love created by imagination like an elusive treasure hiding in places that would make discovery difficult. Tía Lupe was always the anchor that kept me grounded in the reality that the love I was looking for would come—once I was open to it without preconceived notions of what it should be like.

From someone who has long abandoned the hope of finding love, the world can become a quieter, more solitary place—void of the excitement and possibilities that once filled my imagination. But love, in its unpredictable nature, has a way of finding us when we have stopped searching, when we have made peace with being alone. This is the story of a love discovered not through pursuit but through surrendering to peace and tranquility of where we land.

For someone who had given up on the idea of love, I discovered that the heart undergoes a transformation. It builds walls, learns to navigate life without the warmth of romantic affection, and accepts that our journey is meant to be solitary. Days blur into routine, and while there may be a sense of contentment in self-sufficiency, a quiet resignation lingers that something is missing. The idea of love fades into the background—a distant dream from a time when hope seemed brighter and more relentless.

Then, like an unexpected breeze on a still day, love arrives, knocking on our door. It does not come with grand announcements or in the places where one used to search for it. Instead, it emerges from the spaces that were least considered—in a simple moment of kindness or in a shared laugh with a person who was always there, unnoticed in that way. This love is not built on the fantasies of youth, nor does it come with the weight of expectation. It feels different, more authentic, more organic.

When love finds us in this way, it is humbling. There is a realization that all the searching, all the desperation, was not what would bring it to us. Instead, in letting go and accepting ourselves and our circumstances, we created the space for love to enter. And this love feels more sincere, sweeter, because it is unexpected. It is a gift that was never expected but freely given.

For the person who had given up, this love holds a new meaning. It is not about completing oneself but about sharing in the fullness with someone else that already exists. It is the realization that love is not something to be earned or hunted but something that comes naturally when we are truly ready for it—even if we do not know it at the time. It is a reminder that love does not follow rules or timelines; it appears where and when it will, often in the most unanticipated stages of life.

Almost Caught

The eagle flies alone without a mate,
a white pearl floating in an empty sky.
Turquoise Gulf waters, an island of white clouds—
the shadow of a bird in flight with no destination.

Freedom? Alone in flight,
carried by a northern wind.
Endless flight ends as it begins;
the loneliness of freedom becomes a dark shadow.

Every movement magnified,
always watched, never touched—
scientists conduct experiments.
A rare bird lost in flight,
"Stay where you are."

The pursuit of an endless cycle—
life chasing the rising sun,
empty sky and eternity circling the earth.
Foolish fowl, scorched by the promise of free flight.

Blown into dust, chasing the universe.
Time is endless,
return to the nest where it all began.
Your journey will end where you started.

Free and Alone

Today revealed scarring memories
of a wounded heart, alone, silent,
tears in the eye of an explosive storm,
free from human passion.
The pain of a lonely child, alone.
Watching family members on television.
Butterflies of fear dancing
over the fear's uncertainty—
with no love, no sorrow,
no compassion, there is freedom.
As a lonely man, I have become
a companion of freedom
without love.

A New Day

In the shadows of night, eyes burn with a quiet intensity,
embers smoldering with the weight of knowing.
Heartbeats echo, unbound,
a frozen night revealing its quiet truths.
Tears stream softly,
etching paths along flushed cheeks.
Voices rise, fracturing the stillness,
shards of sound scattering across mirrored skies.
Accusations linger in unseen corners,
frozen in the absence of touch.
Silent thoughts churn, muscles coil,
lips ache with the nearness of
what is felt but unspoken.
Arms encircle in a fragile warmth,
spirits meet in a shared burst of life.
Laughter tumbles freely,
love standing steady against the night.
Pain and joy entwine, inseparable,
gifts of connection that time cannot erase.
In the quiet, a family rests,
children's dreams tracing unspoken stories.
Morning rises, its light threading through embraces,
dissolving the weight of darkness.
Whispers of delight ripple softly,
a tender harmony born of shared understanding.
In silence, eyes reflect quiet hopes,
visions of tomorrows shaped by this moment.
Thoughts linger on those absent,
their presence carried forward
in the warmth of dawn.

Star My Friend

On the last plane of the day, a Star arrives,
deboarding the plane,
she glances in my direction,
we notice each other, a contagious smile,
dark oval-shaped eyes
framed by glistening black hair.
Her bronze-colored skin glows
with the aid of the artic sunset,
capturing the Indigenous spirit—
the essence of the past that has remained
untouched.
I capitulate—she is like me,
Aztec and Tlingit ancient Indian souls
decedents of the ancients. We both stare
in wonder at what brought two worlds
to a cold land surrounded by wilderness.
Frozen by time in stillness, her body dances,
releasing the ancient rhythms of the spirits.
I want to dance. My Indian spirit awakens.
With the early spring, we know time is short,
So we take each other's hands and embrace precious minutes.

Plea for Love

We are in the presence of love.
Tears harden like cement
with the fog of laughter
hanging in the air.
Hatred is pounded into
the Foundation of institutions
and voices are sealed in the confined vacuum
of limbo, to never be heard.
We plead to society—
feel, see. and hear our love.
It's a natural gift, and we are sharing it with you.
We have felt, seen, and heard your voice,
and want to share with you and others.
Hatred reverberates across airways,
designated leaders repeat messages of canned evil.
At the cost of a civilized society, the struggle continues,
but righteousness and love will survive.

Alma

Standing before God, family, and friends,
I proclaim my love, my commitment, my pledge—
for the rest of my life, my soul, my truest friend.

Alma, I proclaim my love to you,
the woman I would marry.
To all here today, I reveal my heart,
my spirit dancing with passion.

I admired you long before we loved,
as a professional, a guardian, a mother,
someone to share thoughts and dreams,
someone kind, confident, and full of love.

My life has been blessed with achievements and victories,
opportunities to see the world,
to meet many people,
but none of these can compare to the gift I have received—
the gift of loving you, Alma.

No experience, no victory,
no place or person I have encountered
can replace the blessing I hold in my heart.
Loving you, Alma, is the greatest gift of all.

What Love is Built On

A pairing of values, a quest for love,
but love cannot be sought,
cannot be found.

It cannot be chosen,
nor simply picked.
Love is not taken;
love is not a quest—
love can only be.

Love is not for the timid,
not for the weak.
Love is not planned;
it is a gift, freely given,
with an open spirit.

Love challenges,
love inspires,
love demands,
love confuses.

It is for those with faith and hope;
love must be believed.
love is uncontrolled,
love is strength to the soul,
joy to the spirit.

Love is our eternal life together,
hand in hand,
side by side.
love is our unspoken belief in each other.

I Cielo

Where the mountain meets the sky,
we stand together as soaring spirits.
Where the snowflake touches the earth,
we walk, feeling the coolness and the nourishment.

Where the river meets the sea,
we see our worlds connected,
Souls touched, cultures collide.
Where, somewhere, somebody was looking for me,
where someone found me—

at the mountain's peak, we paused,
waiting for each other.
Where the snowflakes kiss the earth
and the stream meets the sea,
we found comfort, peace, and love.

I heard your voice say hello,
And we stood in silence, waiting to wake from a dream.
Where dreams meet reality, and I met you—
where the softness of your voice soothes, sleep intervenes.

My waking is greeted by your smile,
ever unchanged.
Where time becomes a companion,
distance grows with passion,
and laughter lingers for days, sheltered in our minds.
Where we can soar, En el Cielo.

In Silence

Red eyes in the dark of night,
glowing like hot coals, raging with pain,
a furnace burning.

Heartbeats pound, sounds burst
into a night frozen like an ice cube.
Flowing streams of tears cascade downward,
rose-colored cheeks moistened with sorrow.

Voices clash in objection, breaking
a black-mirrored night, shattering to dust.
It was you—no, it was you! Oh!
When did this happen? I guess I forgot.

As we lay in silence like statues
in an unvisited museum, tears flow.
Random thoughts turn into a concert,
in reflection as moist flesh meets, lips touching.

With arms coiled around each other,
passions and spirits swell into an eruptive
volcano, lava pouring from the center of life.
Laughter follows like children chasing
a parade on the Fourth of July.
Love holds the secrets, a safe, protecting
pains, sorrows, and joys as gifts of love.
We have felt, dwelled, and created passions,
escaping the reality of the morning to come.

Promise

My promise to you, as we walk hand in hand,
sharing our lives together, is to
love you, Victor, and Cassandra,
with all the love that God can inspire.

To always treat you and our children
with the deepest respect,
to offer the warmth of my heart when you are cold,
and be your light and joy when you feel sad or gloomy.

I will always be open and sincere,
even when silence feels easier.
I will speak when words are needed
and never quit on the love that brought us together.

I promise to always remember how our love began,
and to treat our marriage as
an endless romance, an eternal love.

I will be your partner, your lover,
with passion and compassion—always.

Are You Sure?

Bitter winds, dark skies, winter shelters spring—
but will one welcome the other?
A union of seasons, a joining of two.

Are we sure this is what we want?
Are we sure we can even ask the question?

Will winter, in its shelter, prepare spring for its arrival?
Can snow-covered mountains preserve the eternal?

Will premature cherry blossoms hold back
their beauty, waiting for the perfect time?

Will the quiet creek resist boiling over,
its calm flow refreshed by snowmelt as spring races in?

Migratory birds choose their ancient flight;
summer awaits their nests.
Are you sure you want to do this?

Does the salmon fight its way upstream
to create life, knowing death is near?

Does the desert flower reject newfound moisture
when a thunderstorm comes?

Does a random rose repel the hummingbird's visit?
Are you sure you want to do this?

Is it possible to live without prayer,
or without believing in something greater?

Can we live without air, water, or nourishment?
Can there be a world without day and night?

Is there a night sky without a moon
or flickering stars?

Can life spring from the earth without the sun?
Are you sure you want to do this?

When spring comes, there are no answers to these questions.
There is no choice.

In the cycle of life, events unfold without question.

There can be no love without pain,
no laughter without sorrow,
no questions without answers.

When our eyes met, there was no question,
no choice—only love.
Are you sure you want to do this?

The Light

The brilliance of sunlight did not ignite the passion of life.
The vision of you exploded
into a carefree fantasy.

The moonlight did not create the glimmer of unfound love.
The thought of getting to know you aroused butterflies
in my soul.

The twilight's gleam did not stir the amber
smoldering in my heart.
The desire to see you again burst
into an uncontrolled wildfire.

The light of day seemed like any other day
until I saw your light.
The light of your smile as you scanned the room
welcomed new faces.

The light of day seemed ordinary
until I saw your light.
The light of your laughter teased my Mexican face,
smiles dancing in your eyes.

The light of day felt familiar
until I saw your light.
The sparkle in your eye pondered,
"What is possible?"

The light of day seemed like any day
until I saw your light.
the light of honest purity you brought into the room,
Accepting the obvious.

The light of your intellect challenged
every corner of reality—
You introduced your light
into an ordinary day.

Aztec Princess

Long, curly hair in shades of brown and black,
the desert wind cuts through silken strands,
north wind blowing toward an unknown future.

Aztec ancestors whisper in your shadow,
defying the ancient prophecy—
successor to the ancient Sun Queen,
possessing ancestral blood.

Royalty, holding cities in your palm,
dignity, breathing life into the walking dead.
Prophecy points the way:
New cities and ancient temples rise.
An Aztec princess has been spotted in Mission, Texas!

Together Bound

In a starlit ballet, intertwining souls connect,
minds collide, souls explore, a celestial blaze erupts.
Unforeseen visions, reckless passion,
a splattering of turquoise hues—
the waters protecting Tulum.
A lover's maze, our embrace, a fervent grip,
a force unknown.

A vise binding us tight,
pressure implodes the universe,
an uncontrollable allure,
navigating twilight's unscheduled voyages
through time's embrace, exploring each other's future
through memories guiding our future
with accumulated knowledge form the past
passed to the inheritors of the new race with grace.

Memories unfold, the past flows into the present,
a love story retold.
Beneath a full moon, spring's sweet revelation,
our meeting transcends the ancestral past.

As seasons pass, seeds of love take root,
from the past, a future in passion's pursuit—
growing into lasting dreams.
Laughter echoes, a melody of joy,
our hearts intertwined, soul-baring love reveals
each other's past, paving a path to the future.

A sacred vow, passion-filled, agreed upon
in the cup of shared pain and boundless joy,
we drink from this common cup—
our love, without restriction,
past lives intertwined. Future generations blessed.
Our love story, a timeless, passionate quest.

Valentine's Day

It was just yesterday—I held a card in my hand,
displaying circus tents and baby elephants,
Valentine's Day—a moment to share over a lifetime.

Playing dodgeball and hopscotch,
dancing in a cafeteria,
dreams of chasing girls,
chasing their innocent shadows,
watching a kiss walk away.

Life converges my days into one—
airports and phone booths,
long-distance childhood love still growing.
Where is the playground?
Where are the children playing?
Are they still chasing innocent shadows?

Time becomes an image;
children's faces turn and look back—
soon, tomorrow will become yesterday.

Mi Vida

Voices race through space at fiber-optic speed,
creating a modern romance from distant lands online.

Tele-courting, dancing an electronic dance of first acquaintance—
"Who is she, and what is her name? Will she laugh at my wit?
Can she tell I am sensitive?
She has a southern name.

"If you could give me any name, what name would I be given?"

With the grace of a mariposa,
You pollinate happiness in others.
"If you could have any other name, it would be Vida,
Vida—that which you give to others."

What is in a name?
You have a southern name, a name from south of the border.
Do I dare to say mi Vida?

What's In a Southern Name?

She flung her irresistible laughter
like an uncontrolled virus, infecting everyone with joy.
Her head tilted to the side, hair swirling around her face,
sun-blushed cheeks glowing in the night.

Black strands of hair conceal the edges of her eyes,
a fragile, porcelain-skinned face delivers a smile,
soliciting a stolen kiss.

Laughter fractures the silence—
"Hey, what's so funny? Why are you laughing?"
"Oh, me too!"
We trade the seriousness of life for impulsive moments,
the joy of exchange, mutual reactions.

Laughter from a forgotten childhood when we knew each other—
making fun of each other.

"Do you like to joke around? You make me laugh.
You are so funny."

A measure of caution whispered to a childhood friend—
"She seems nice, but you never know."
"We can't be serious all the time."

Her voice soothes the tension,
rigid muscles relax, and a grin is revealed.

"Who are you, and what is your name?"

"Alma is my name. It is a southern name,
A southern name from the land of the border—
The border between taking life too seriously
and achieving happiness."

An invisible boundary has been discovered,
between seriousness and laughter—
a new friend north of the border with a southern name,
a lifetime conversation without a name.

We both rose from the Border, both with Southern names.

When We Knew Each Other

In a forgotten world, we met by accident.
Pyramids, standing sentinels, protected the stars,
pointing toward our universe's origin.
A new beginning—
an abandoned city left as a gift by forgotten people,
ancients who danced on their toes, arms stretched toward the night sky,
touching the moon that would bring the sun.

Our pyramids!
A civilization embracing with strength the future—prophesied!
A thousand cultures kneeling in prayer.
We drifted away from each other on a river
with two forks toward two worlds.

One world with blue eyes, of the time of conquest
gazed into my dark eyes, of the Indian soul
bronze skin glistening with the sweat of labor.
Another world with dark opal eyes
welcomed you into its breast with the sweet milk of Mother Earth.

Ages passed as calendars were chiseled in stone,
granite sentinels of ancient memories accumulated.
Time, the wall between our passions,
crumbled by the faith of a thousand cultures.

Touching fingertip to fingertip,
explosions of sunbursts hurled together
as we stared into each other's eyes—
a childhood innocence pounding in our hearts.
Laughter, we ran as children, chasing around trees,
running through cornfields, touching lips,
a Mestizo is born. Forever!

Seasons Change

A gentle breeze sheds golden leaves,
floating across a gray sky, the chill in the wind departs.
It is time, greeting the bite of winter's frozen breath,
ice crystals dancing, chasing the days of advancing time,
waiting for spring rains to arrive suddenly.

An abundance of needed moisture, the last drop of spring rain,
greets summer; life begins with ease, greenery erupts.
Sporadic blue skies reveal the sun's passion until
summer awakens—open arms in a life-giving embrace,
with a gentle sway, a whispering breeze,
announcing life's possibilities.

Sun-kissed days, crimson hues,
painted sunset skies in shades of orange, red, and blue—
nature's masterpiece crafted daily.
Summer birds sing, bouncing monarchs float
from blossom to blossom, sweet aromas bloom.
Life's creation unfolds, moment by moment.

With laughter and joy in every space,
distant children's laughter echoes in planted fields,
tree to tree, rivers water overflowing green pastures,
flowers in bloom; thunderstorms burst, awakening nature's
slumber.
Silent dreams pierce hearts, evening stars in our eyes,
summer's song is written.
We find peace, a moment of bliss,
brought by a brilliant sunrise; we see hope.

Open hearts reveal our place—
living is easy in summer's glory,
bathing in its warmth
with the sun in my face,
relentless anxiety fades.

Mankind's Universe

Seasons cycle, autumn hues give way to winter's chill,
greeting winter rains, the warmth of sunrise replaces the cold,
cooling sunsets repeat, waiting for long summer days without end—
clear skies, dancing stars streak across the horizon.

Change and transformation occur in the vastness of space;
each revolution reveals fate.
Life transforms, and a symphony of existence unfolds,
destinies created as crises emerge with every spin of the colossal universe.

Shadows dance upon the earth, and tumultuous ordeals unfold.
Wars echo in a cacophony of violence and strife,
mutilating the fabric of society, weaving a tapestry of life,
evolution continues relentlessly.

Unwritten laws stand as silent sentinels,
protecting life's delicate balance.
neglecting nature's cries,
objections confined to the whims of power and lies.

Schools become messengers,
indoctrinating young minds, shaping perspectives,
molding nature's future, bending its bounds.
Yet amid the chaos, despair lies—a plea in the wind,
a collective prayer.

The merry-go-round creaks, collapsing under decay,
a plea to the Universe: "Show us the way!"
Yelling and screaming, voices of the young rise in desperation,
our carousel of existence faces disintegration.

We seek resolution, gazing into the cosmic expanse,
where stars are born, sparkling with hope,

brilliant in a celestial dance.
We search for answers; who is listening?
Is the universe hiding its elusive repair kit
in a cosmic toolbox? Can we find a perfect fit?

Guide us to the solutions, cosmic engineer—
mend the fractures, quiet the voices of fear,
a cosmic lesson awaits.
Let curiosity be the glue binding our wounds,
creating a world anew.

CHAPTER 6
What is Next?

In the early mornings, just before sunrise, I woke to the feeling of a cool dirt floor under my bare feet of the small adobe house built by my grandparents in northern Mexico. The moist, earthy touch of the clay under my feet was a stark reminder of how far my journey has been. Back then, we had so little—no insulation against the cold or the heat, there was enough work to keep us going. From that humble beginning, my learning began, a life experience that would span borders, cultures, and expectations.

As a boy, working alongside my family in the fields, I watched my father's hands crack and callous under the sun. We shared what little we had in the evenings over a campfire, and my elders spoke of a dream—a vision of a better life that I could scarcely imagine. When we migrated to the U.S., we moved often, following the seasons and the harvests. I was enrolled in an all-White high school as one of the few students of Mexican descent. The halls were lined with pristine lockers, but I felt the weight of otherness in forever gazing over the horizon and daydreaming with every moment of silence. While others assumed my place was back in the fields, I found myself drawn to books, determined to understand my story, and struggling to write a new chapter.

Through years of work and study, I learned how to move through the layers of a society where people like me often faced steep challenges. As a Chicano, I confronted the assumptions that came with my last name, my background, and my accent, always pushing through the socioeconomic layers that separated me from the mainstream. Racism and discrimination were not occasional barriers; they were like walls that rose up, one after another. But I learned to overcome them, to press forward anyway. I entered rooms where I felt unwelcome and took on roles where people questioned my worth before I learned to speak out and keep going. I realized my journey was not just about my success; it was about paving a way for others, those who looked and sounded like me but had not had the same opportunities.

In the 1960s and 70s, as the winds of social change swept through America, I felt the pull. As a proud Chicano, I joined the marches and protests, my voice lifted with those calling for justice and equity. The chants and songs echoed in my memory, symbols of unity and strength. The movement grounded me in my culture and my purpose; I realized I did not just want a seat at the table—I wanted to change the table itself.

After serving in the military, I worked in both the private and public sectors, carving out a reputation as a leader who listened, a voice for those often ignored. But I knew I needed something more to make a real difference. I pushed myself to new heights, pursuing a bachelor's degree at the University of Oregon, a master's degree at Harvard, and completing my Ph.D. coursework. Harvard was a world away from the dusty fields of my youth, but it was there I refined my vision of what should and could be. Surrounded by ambitious minds and lofty ideals, I realized the profound value of my journey.

Years later, I worked for two U.S. presidents, drawing from a well of resilience and understanding that was as rare as it was impactful. But now, as I look around at a country where national leaders have returned to promoting fear and hatred of immigrants. I wonder what lies in store for a former migrant farm worker—a Chicano who made his way through hard work, who rose from dirt floors to ivy walls and Capitol Hill. What is the future for someone like me, who has already lived out the "American Dream" only to find that it is being threatened and torn down?

And in my heart, I know that the answer is not about me. It

is about the people who still toil in fields, the young Chicanos who can still hear in their classrooms what I once heard: that they do not belong, that they do not have a future here. The future for a Chicano like me lies not only in personal success but in the strength to keep pushing and changing the narrative. It is in showing that the obstacles we face today are not new—they are just another layer. And if I have climbed them before, then maybe, just maybe, I can keep helping others climb them, too.

Now, I reflect on this journey in my home—a large house with a pool and all the comforts I once thought impossible. From dirt floors to Ivy League halls, from the quiet desperation of my youth to the pride of a life spent fighting for a better world. I am still that boy with calloused hands and big dreams. And my story? It is far from over. The future belongs to those of us who refuse to give up.

The solution for hearts that have crossed the border lies not in the past but in the future. Mexico's soul must reach beyond its artificial borders, fulfilling its prophetic destiny by reclaiming its lost tribes. It is the fate of all who have dared to straddle both worlds, who seek to dismantle the walls. The border has severed families and estranged us from the motherland. Bridges must be built to unite those willing to embark on this journey of the spirit. Soon, the ancient language of forgotten tribes, once spoken under the sun, shall resound once more, united as one.

To Survive

As the tree blossoms, fruit sprouts on the tree,
ready for the hungry to consume.
Appetites for Aztec scriptures are lost in storms long subsided,
but we can harvest the new thoughts of our sons and daughters,
provide tools for those who have not farmed.
Anger and Fear become our allies as reconstruction races
against the wind.
Shelters built for the wanderers of forgotten emotions.
Here, take and learn from what is being offered.

The Mother

The heavens are opening
to share the secrets of eternity.
But no one is there to listen.
Where have you gone, Mother? People are dying—
others are walking around dead!
The thumping of your soulful heart
is heard by humanity.
Their fear of the unknown
Exposed for all to see—
but you already know.
Make us fear you no more, come,
come to heal humanity and
make us a part of your plan.
So our breath will be one.

Life

Listen to the sacred mother's cry.
She mourns for the loss of life,
how all living things on our blue planet,
are threatened by ignorance—
ignorance of how we humans rely on connections
binding us to the energy that surrounds every living thing
Mother Earth displays her anger.
Winds of destruction are a warning,
but fire sterilizes and nourishes the land
rain clears and cleanses contaminated soil
earth breaks open to reconfigure disrupted lands
as Mother Earth struggles to regain what was.
There's still life in her soul,
life giving life to all living organisms.
Birds fly without restriction.
Plants grow from enriching soil.
Humanity feeds off the land.
People have died giving their lives,
so everything left behind is precious.
New life stops to stare.
The earth is alive with cries of despair.
Her stability and sustainability threatened—
what was, will never be again.

Shadow of Wisdom

Stop to kiss the shadow that follows you,
constant companion by your side,
a breath away following you,
close enough to feel by touch.
The warmth of your footsteps
pave the way on an unknown path.
Why does this secret shadow person follow?
Its movements synchronized
in constant rhythm with your own,
The shadow person will never speak.
Our shadows reside everywhere.
Silent and dark, a transparent being,
keeper of the meaning of man's existence,
knower of good and evil,
holder of the confidence
they stole from us.

Origins of Chicomoztoc

The golden rays of an eastern sunrise
reveal the glimmering reflection
of a snow-covered valley,
dormant from cultivation, abandoned.

The land of the seven caves birthed Aztlan,
Mother Earth nurtured the Mexica people,
seven tribes of Nahuatl voices dispersed over three continents.
From seven caves rose an advanced civilization,
where all learned, art, science, and astronomy.
They built roads, stretching across the land,
cities, linking hearts and diverse cultures.

Yet a prophecy loomed: an invasion of angry men,
rootless souls with empty hearts, haunted by the spirit
of their own cruelty. Led by pale-skinned warriors,
their fiery red hair ablaze, deep, sea-blue colored eyes
faces hidden beneath long, tangled beards,
masking misled intentions.
They came with a fury inhuman and cold,
tearing families apart, stealing women,
making temporary unions, temporary satisfaction—
The invaders' dark seed sown.

They were strangers posing as friends,
arriving to uproot a centuries-old civilization.
With intentions to expand their religion
by force and violence, they stole gold
from ancient temples. Driven by the intoxication
of wealth, blind to the cost, deaf to cries of
an ancient people pleading to be preserved.
Ancient tribes invaded; families separated.

They were forced to wander across the continents,
marching north across barren lands,
to wait for the time to return home.
The time is now! They have returned!
To the place of Origin, to Chicomoztoc, to face the invaders!
Rise up, Aztlan!

Antiquity

We walk on the cobblestones of antiquity,
revisiting the ancestral land.
These narrow streets were witness to angry revolutions
The pursuit of freedom, a history preserved in stone
past lives, struggles, victory in defeat,
celebrations of freedom, a common cause
bound by a belief, a vision of equality.
Ancient philosophy guides the righteous minds of the people,
giving hope to the have-nots and the forgotten,
creating a place for all to be heard,
a community without fear
a future where daughters and sons
walk the same cobblestones in peace.
Voices embedded into the ancient stones
scream for everyone to hear.
Don't forget why, don't forget the dream!
The struggle continues, but we find hope.

Chicano of the Past

The days of rebellion live as memories now,
echoes of Chicano resistance surging
against injustice, racism, discrimination—
a fierce ancestral force driving us forward,
asking only to be seen, heard, included
in the promise of America's future.
A future dreamed by evening campfires,
as smoke rose through jungle canopies,
drifting into shadows of what might come.
Aztec prophecies sketched our paths northward,
across rivers dividing continents, deserts stretching,
over a wall of snow-covered peaks.
We crossed the great snow without guidance,
no compass but the spark of hope,
driven to forge a future, to build anew.
Generations passed; the Chicano struggle endured,
modern-day Aztec warriors facing adversity con ganas.
Now, the aging middle-class Chicano sits,
startled awake by rhetoric of a familiar past:
A door, once sealed by resistance, has been reopened.
Ancient warriors stir under ancestral tombs,
whispering to the aging Chicano: Rise once more!
Never relent to society's pressure to forget—
we are one people, woven to become
the many, bound to this land unbroken.

Breaking News

Sitting in the safety of a middle-class home,
behind closed gates, trimmed lawns, HOA rules,
watching network news—proclamations
of an invasion across the U.S.-Mexico border.
Alarms ring, warning of a broken border,
and fear stirs a call for walls, for barriers.
"Stop the invasion," cry self-anointed voices of power.
A spark flares, spreading like wildfire—
a wave of angry words, clenched fists,
attacks on families, places of worship,
the sanctity of private homes shattered.
Violence cuts through society's restraints,
shattering a silence that once held so long.
Screams from households once quiet rise,
loud enough to shake the sixty-five-inch screen,
loud enough to rattle what was once so distant,
and for a moment, the quiet is a contradiction.
Where all was once contained, palatable,
I find myself awakening, rising from silence,
memories of progress unraveling before me.
I am choked by words I cannot speak,
by the confines of this well-ordered room,
bound by laws, by social rules, by restraint.
What will it take to shake loose
from the lessons of my elders?
"Don't make waves, mijo," they'd say,
as if silence would keep us afloat,
as an unseen riptide pulls us under
no matter how hard we swim.
The pressure to stay quiet weighs on my chest,
as if silence itself could make me safe.
But news stories reach me, quietly relentless,
of unexpected knocks on doors, demanding hands,
agents in dark uniforms forcing entry

into the homes of grandparents, of aunts and uncles,
like a storm battering down doors,
rifling through their personal histories,
turning old photos and trinkets into evidence
against lives lived here for generations,
in lands they walked barefoot as children,
familiar with every dusty road, every mesquite tree.
Their roots run deeper than memory,
stretching back more than a thousand years,
woven into the soil, the mountains, the rivers.
Their only offense: a lineage written in their bones,
the color of their skin, the accent of their words,
the mere fact of being Mexican—
an identity I carry, too, here in this quiet room,
in the safety of these walls.
So, what will it take to rise,
to unlearn the quiet that keeps me still?
I can wait no longer. The time is here!

Time to Change

Grounded in the spirit of the ancients.
rooted in ancient past,
and guided by lessons from a conquest,
we stand as one.
A union bound in reverence
for our Mother Earth as we walk her paths,
breathe her air, drink her water,
and use her fire to warm us.
In our return to Aztlan, she moves closer
to a fifth reckoning—a shift,
a stirring of land and of her children.
We wait to understand this path,
guided by the deep spirits of Indigenous souls.
Each assault on the original peoples
echoes across sacred lands,
as Mother Earth remembers,
answers, with wind, water, and fire.
Now, a rumbling warns—
justice poised for those who tread
on her children or disregard her gifts.
A remedy stirs, borne of love,
compassion, and awakening.
A revival of ancient wisdom.
How to live in harmony—not just with the earth
and her creatures, but with each other.
We've known the strength of acceptance,
and lost the art of learning from our oppressors.
As attacks persist, these lessons are tested:
listen to learn, to understand, to accept.
It is time to resist, reflect, and act with purpose.
We will gather wisdom as we go.
It is time to awaken those ready to adapt,
to seek out those with the courage to embrace
the teachings of understanding,

of living in harmony—with Mother Earth
as our anchor, and community as our home,
standing firm in the power to think,
and to love others as ourselves.

Toward the Sun of Huitzilopochtli

The sacred footsteps of the Mexica
reverberate through Teotihuacan's ancient stones.
Echoes rise within the temples and pyramids,
summoning the fire of gods once honored.
Heartbeats quicken with each stride,
the spirit's journey bound by sacred tension,
drawn ever nearer to Tonatiuh, the Sun Eternal,
whom our ancestors revered in flame and blood.
On sacred trails, the pathways have narrowed,
guided and strained, each step aflame—
the journey shaped by sacrifice and devotion,
leading toward the radiant Sun of Life.
In the light of truth, under the weight of sincerity,
we ascend, embracing the ancient call.
I am on the path, in the true spirit of our people,
toward the Sun of Life, with a full heart.
Offering peaceful hope for the future.
We are home, a place with many colors,
language, and ceremonies, watched over
by Huitzilopochtli, keeper of the sun.

Daybreak

Standing against the morning breeze,
I silently stare into the horizon,
waiting for the life-giving sunrise.
Dust rises from the tilled field,
neat precision rows cultivated,
ready to deliver life.
A stirred morning breeze spreads
across the empty, waiting fields
as the hands of harvest arrive.
As the dust gathers on my eyelids,
a mountain breeze sweeps the cultivated valley,
clearing my vision.
I realize the power of time—
what was foretold, what has been, and
what will be. The sun will rise for my people.

Infinite

Think! That someday this will happen.
It has happened before!
The chain of life is revolving;
soon the future
will overcome the past into infinity.
Having been here before,
time will overcome what will be.
Going on to another someday,
overcoming once more to
what will be in the future again.
We have been here before.

Freedom Found

Decades have passed, distant horizons revealed,
worlds collided, cultures clashed, and lands transformed.
A never-ending quest, adventures still pending—
civilizations unfinished, under construction,
but hope lingers on the horizon, a better place yet to be built.

We wander, endlessly searching,
no specific destination, no place to call home—
no predetermined path, but the freedom to choose
our land, our place, our home.
Hope glimmers beyond the snow-covered mountains,
endless waterfalls and streams flow through decades past,
distant horizons watched over by the ancients,
Nurtured by nature itself.

Fear chases, seeking relief—
pain, families lost, civilizations abandoned.
Yet still, hope waits on the horizon—
freedom lies just beyond.
A never-ending quest, a never-ending horizon—
fear of pain, insane love, the loss of freedom—
But hope always lies ahead.

Imprisoned adventures, imprisoned freedom,
but still, hope is on the horizon,
Endless adventures await, freedom forever sought.
Decades have passed, countless horizons crossed—
Now, peace lies in the present.
Hope is found, a place to belong—
on the horizon, freedom is found.

CONCLUSION

Some might say my journey, chronicled in poetry, is unique, and it certainly is. But others have traveled similar roads and overcome obstacles as great or greater than mine—men and woman from all cultures around the globe. I hope the stories in this book honor all who have navigated various migrations and resettlements yet retained a passion for their ancestral homelands. As I mentioned in the introduction of this book, we all should embrace the diverse threads that define our shared humanity. No matter where we find ourselves today, our souls (and our DNA) are anchored in the historical past.

It is a past worth knowing and honoring.

Have you ever wondered about your deepest roots? If so, I encourage you to research genealogical records and history books as well as the tales told by your parents, grandparents, aunts, and uncles. These memories can often be traced through generations of ancestors who understood the truths of the past and preserved them for you to discover today. It may take years to uncover the lore, legend, and prophecies fulfilled or still pending. Exploration requires tenacity and unquenched curiosity. But I can assure you that sleuthing has a great purpose and will expand your personal horizons.

You will excavate answers to questions you have held your whole life, and you will step into the future more prepared to achieve the mission into which you were born. You will better understand how and why you were destined to arrive at this precise time and place on Mother Earth.

Who knows...perhaps you will be called to include the distant past in your memoir one day, as I did with *A Fly in Milk*. Perhaps you will write a companion book of poetry, both for cathartic value and to further share your experiences with other seekers.

No matter your destiny, I wish you well as you connect the past with your present purpose. Be all you are meant to be with the blessings of your forebearers.

ABOUT THE AUTHOR

Victor Vasquez was born in 1949 into a family of migrant workers from Eagle Pass, Texas. As a child, he was grounded in the lifestyle of Northern Mexico in communities such as Piedras Negras, Monterey, and Saltillo. He learned the ancient lore of his people while gathering around campfires in the evenings with his family and traveling the West and Pacific Northwest harvesting crops. He juxtaposed these experiences against life in Oregon, where he attended his first school and where his father eventually settled the family and enrolled Victor in a predominantly White elementary school.

Integrating into English-only academics was a struggle, and integrating into an unfamiliar culture was even more challenging. Poverty, prejudice, an absent mother, an overworked father, and dependent siblings had Victor working odd jobs from an early age to help support the family. A stint in junior high with a committed art teacher and high school sports helped counterbalance a rebellious streak as he made his way toward graduation, only to be told by a school counselor that he was not "college material." He recalls being told that he might consider trade school and becoming a mechanic.

Victor proved the school counselor wrong by enrolling in Blue Mountain Community College, enlisting, and serving honorably in the Army as his father and uncles had, and graduating from the University of Oregon. He earned a master's degree at Harvard University's Kennedy School of Government and, over the span of thirty years, became a public servant serving two presidential administrations. He worked his way up from writing briefing books for the White House to Deputy Assistant Secretary of Defense for the Office of the Secretary and Deputy Under Secretary in Rural Development for the Department of Agriculture. His focus was fighting poverty across the country, supporting rural communities in the Mississippi Delta, the Appalachia region that provided energy needs for decades and was later abandoned, and the Southwest border region—his place of origin where over two-thirds of the Latinos in the U.S. reside, as well as the Native American community that is often forgotten.

Today, Victor studies the roots of his lineage and prophecies stretching back to Aztec rule. Within his autofiction, *A Fly In Milk (Una Mosca En La Leche)*, he shares original poetry and ponders the state of humanity, wondering when his ancient people will finally be called home.

www.ingramcontent.com/pod-product-compliance
Lightning Source LLC
Chambersburg PA
CBHW070449050426
42451CB00015B/3409